GREGORY M. DONLEY

The Cleveland Museum of Art
ART SPACES

THE CLEVELAND MUSEUM OF ART

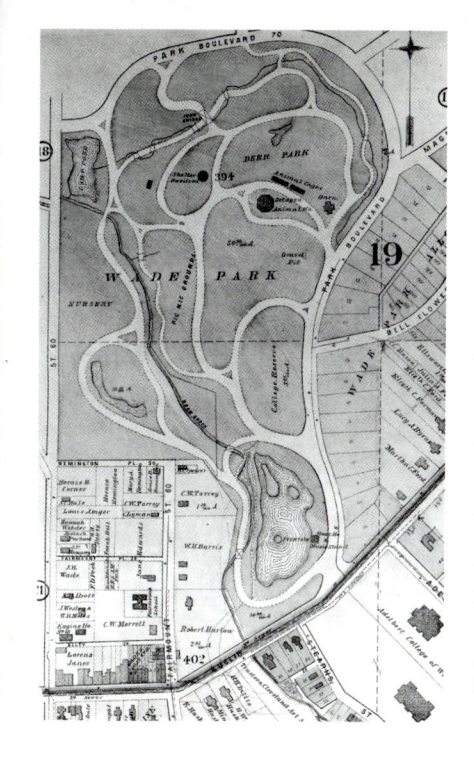

The Cleveland Museum of Art

When the Cleveland Museum of Art opened in 1916, its home city was at the height of explosive growth. The northeastern corner of Ohio, annexed by the state of Connecticut as its Western Reserve in the aftermath of the American Revolution, had been gradually settled beginning around 1800 by New Englanders in search of more and better land. The soil was fertile, the rocks were few, and the climate was temperate—and because of proximity to both Appalachian coal fields and the Great Lakes and Mississippi River watersheds, the location proved favorable not only for agriculture, but

← The Fine Arts Garden and the museum seen from a nearby rooftop, 2013.

← Map depicting Wade Park before the construction of the original museum.

↑ Position of the proposed museum building drawn over a photograph of the site.

→ The 1916 building under construction.

soon enough also for shipping and industry. Over the course of the nineteenth century, waves of immigrants from Germany, Ireland, Italy, Eastern Europe, and the southern United States came to dig canals, load steamers, build railroads, run factories, and fuel the burgeoning service and cultural sectors. By the turn of the century, Cleveland was the sixth-largest city in the country, with a million residents.

The area spawned not only manufacturing, but also innovation, coming from such luminaries as Albert Michelson and Edward Morley (experiments with the speed of light that underpin modern physics), Thomas Edison (light bulb), Harvey Firestone (pneumatic tire), Garrett Morgan (traffic light and gas mask), and Henry Timken (roller bearing). A town of such stature and creative flair, civic leaders agreed, should have a great art museum. Jeptha H. Wade II, heir to the Western Union Telegraph fortune, had already donated a bucolic parkland site for just such a purpose, and his generosity, coordinated with that of three other founding philanthropists—John Huntington, Hinman B. Hurlbut, and Horace Kelley—helped realize the dream with a fine

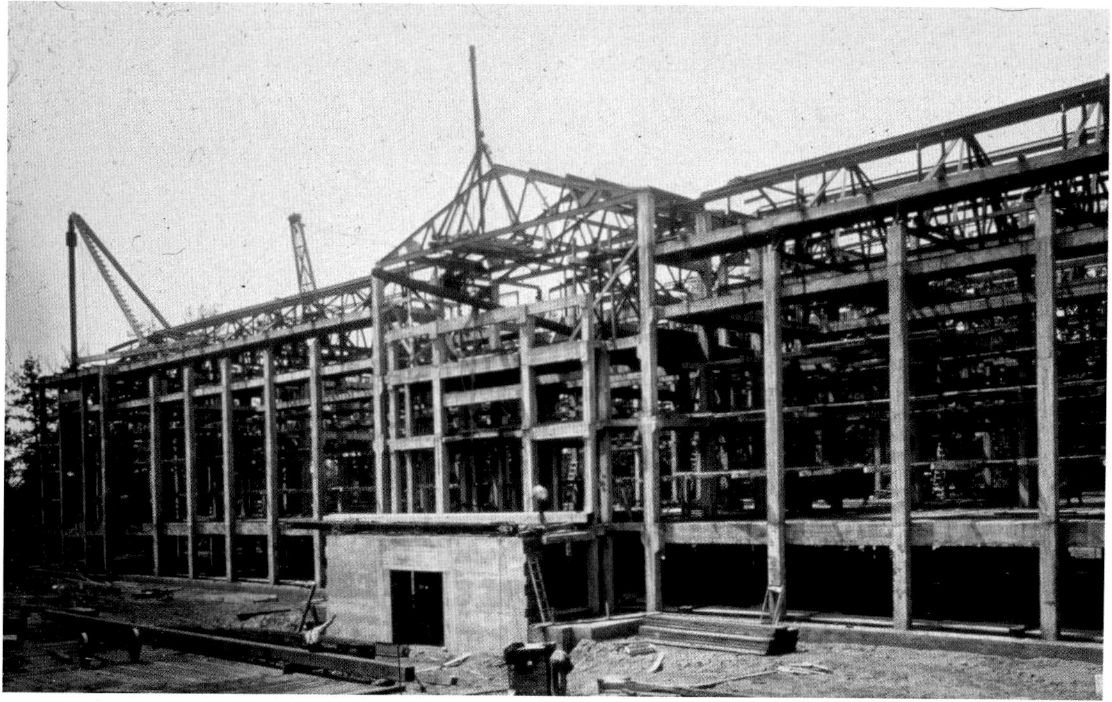

6 / THE CLEVELAND MUSEUM OF ART

Beaux Arts building designed by Cleveland architects Hubbell and Benes. The park site itself was beautiful, but when the Fine Arts Garden designed by the Olmsted Brothers was completed in 1928, it became a truly sublime landscape setting, with the museum facade reflected in the lagoon, framed by lush foliage and sculpture.

The Connoisseur's Museum

The new museum followed the established model of a comprehensive collection housed in a neoclassical edifice, as exemplified by institutions in such cities as Chicago, Buffalo, New York, and Boston. But very early on, a difference emerged in Cleveland: rather than building its holdings by bringing in large intact collections, the Cleveland Museum of Art more often acquired its collection object by object, its curators and director choosing works of art on individual merit. This approach was made possible by the creation of various funds dedicated to art purchase that were established in the decades after the museum's founding, culminating in the $34 mil-

← 1928 flower procession.

↑ A 1958 addition created an outdoor courtyard.

→ The 1958 addition seen from the northeast.

→ Another addition completed in 1983 added gallery space and a new home for the Ingalls Library.

lion cash bequest of Leonard C. Hanna Jr. in 1958. These funds solidified the museum's art-purchase endowment, guaranteeing that subsequent directors and curators would always have the means to make significant acquisitions. Today, nearly half the income from the museum's endowment is dedicated to the purchase of art. The highly selective approach to acquisitions—quality over quantity—continues to this day, resulting in a museum experience that is comprehensive in scope but also manageable in scale. Yet despite the relative restraint, the museum's success and expansion eventually presented challenges.

Adding On: 1958, 1971, and 1983

The founders had a simple plan: build a stately building, fill it with great art, and open the doors. They may never have imagined that the number of visitors each year could exceed half a million, or that a connoisseur's collection could grow to more than 40,000 objects, or that education programs would serve 200,000 annually, or that amenities such as a café and museum store would take on increasing significance in the visitor's experience. Through additions built in 1958, 1971, and 1983, the original structure evolved into a mosaic of buildings. The 1958 addition, designed in the low-key International style by Cleveland architects Hays & Ruth, doubled gallery space by creating, at the north and west of the 1916 building, a square circuit of galleries and offices that also formed a new outdoor courtyard.

By the late 1960s, more space was needed again, especially for education programs, music, and art conservation. Director Sherman E. Lee and the museum leadership were impressed by Marcel Breuer's building for New York's Whitney Museum of American Art and hired the Hungarian-born architect. Unlike the Hays & Ruth addition, the gray-and-black-striped granite cladding and monumental mass of rectangular forms in Breuer's building for Cleveland created a bold statement of contrast: modernity responding to what came before. The 1971 wing added gallery space, an auditorium of more than 700 seats, lecture and recital halls, classrooms, and education staff offices. It also allowed the museum, for the first time, to present in its galleries

↑ Marcel Breuer's education wing with Isamu Noguchi sculpture in the foreground.

↑ The Breuer education wing under construction.

→ School groups convene for lunch on the south steps and terrace.

Western art history from ancient art to the present in chronological sequence. The Asian collections, meanwhile, found a home in a renovated former auditorium in the basement and first level of the 1916 building. The 1983 addition brought another suite of galleries and a comprehensive library facility, which allowed the Ingalls Library to vacate its previous home on the upper floor of the 1958 building and conservation laboratories to be established there.

Lost in Art

Each addition pulled the museum's center of gravity to the north and west. The heart of the original building, its grand rotunda and garden and armor courts, became the periphery as the primary entrance shifted to the education wing. The sequence of galleries, as in many museums, was configured as a single winding path (with a few detours), leading to a visitor experience that was often likened to negotiating a maze. Because of pressures to maximize wall space for art display and minimize potentially damaging light exposure, nearly every exterior window in the original building was covered and very few new ones were included in the additions. This further frustrated navigation.

Imagining the Twenty-First-Century Museum

In the late 1990s, the museum commissioned the firm Cooper Robertson & Partners to produce a facilities master plan. The essence of the firm's report was that the museum needed more gallery space, better laboratory and art-storage space, and a more efficient organization of key functions. Many of the electrical, plumbing, and air handling systems also needed to be updated or replaced. Meeting these practical needs would be a fundamental assignment presented to the architects competing to win the museum project, but there was another requirement as well, one related to the museum's founding concept. Jeptha Wade had donated land for an art museum to be built "for the benefit of all the people forever." The design must help make the museum relevant to the citizens of greater Cleveland, and to wel-

Viñoly's proposal for a new World Trade Center. →

come them all. By 2001 four finalists emerged in the architects' competition: Sir Norman Foster, Frank Gehry, I. M. Pei, and Rafael Viñoly; in September, the museum announced the selection of Viñoly as project architect.

Viñoly's Vision

The museum and its public got to know Rafael Viñoly. Born in 1944 in Montevideo, Uruguay, he spent his early years there and in Buenos Aires, Argentina, where his father was the artistic director of the Sodre Opera Theatre and a noted filmmaker. Viñoly considered a professional career in music before turning his attention to architecture. He attended the University of Buenos Aires, where he brought together five older colleagues to form the influential Estudio de Arquitectura. In 1979 he immigrated to the United States and soon after established a studio in New York City. Today, the firm Rafael Viñoly Architects PC also has offices in London, Tokyo, and Buenos Aires.

One of the distinguishing characteristics of Viñoly's work has been his ingenious and sensitive way of re-

← Visitors in the pre-renovation Asian galleries.

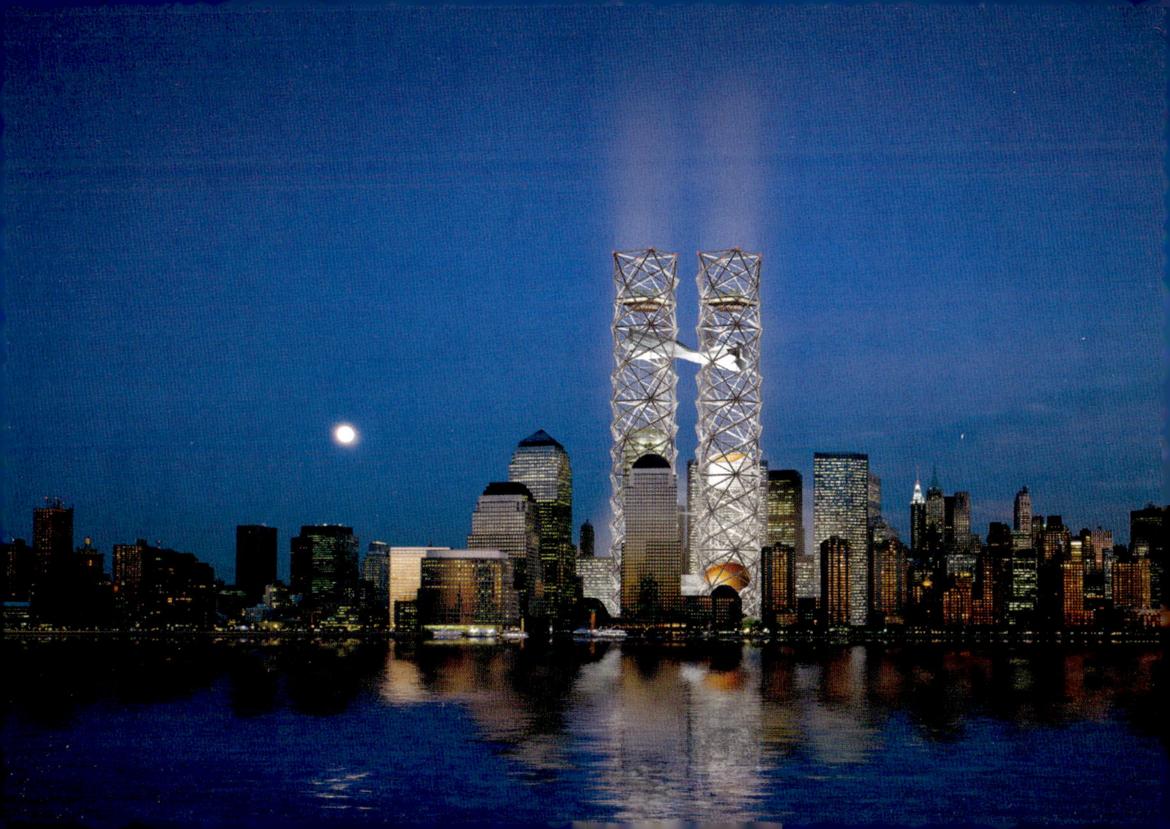

Viñoly's Kimmel Center in Philadelphia.→

↑ Cleveland Museum of Art board chairman Michael Horvitz and architect Rafael Viñoly chat at the official ground-breaking ceremony, 2005.

sponding to a bewildering variety of sites, all the while retaining a signature repertoire of forms: sweeping glass walls, elegant stonework, and graceful, sail-like rooflines. Viñoly finds ways to respect the existing architecture and play to the strengths of a site's natural and built topography, from the gigantic Tokyo International Forum meshing comfortably with its confined urban surroundings, to Philadelphia's Kimmel Center with its symphony hall and program facilities gathered under a single, block-long barrel vault of glass, to the International Research Institute for Climate Prediction, a Columbia University facility in Palisades, New York, lying low along the crest of a ridge, its fieldstone walls and cedar timbers harmonizing quietly with the wooded hilltop site. In the years immediately following his announcement as the Cleveland Museum of Art's architect, a Viñoly-designed convention center opened in Pittsburgh and his design was a finalist in the competition for a new World Trade Center in New York City.

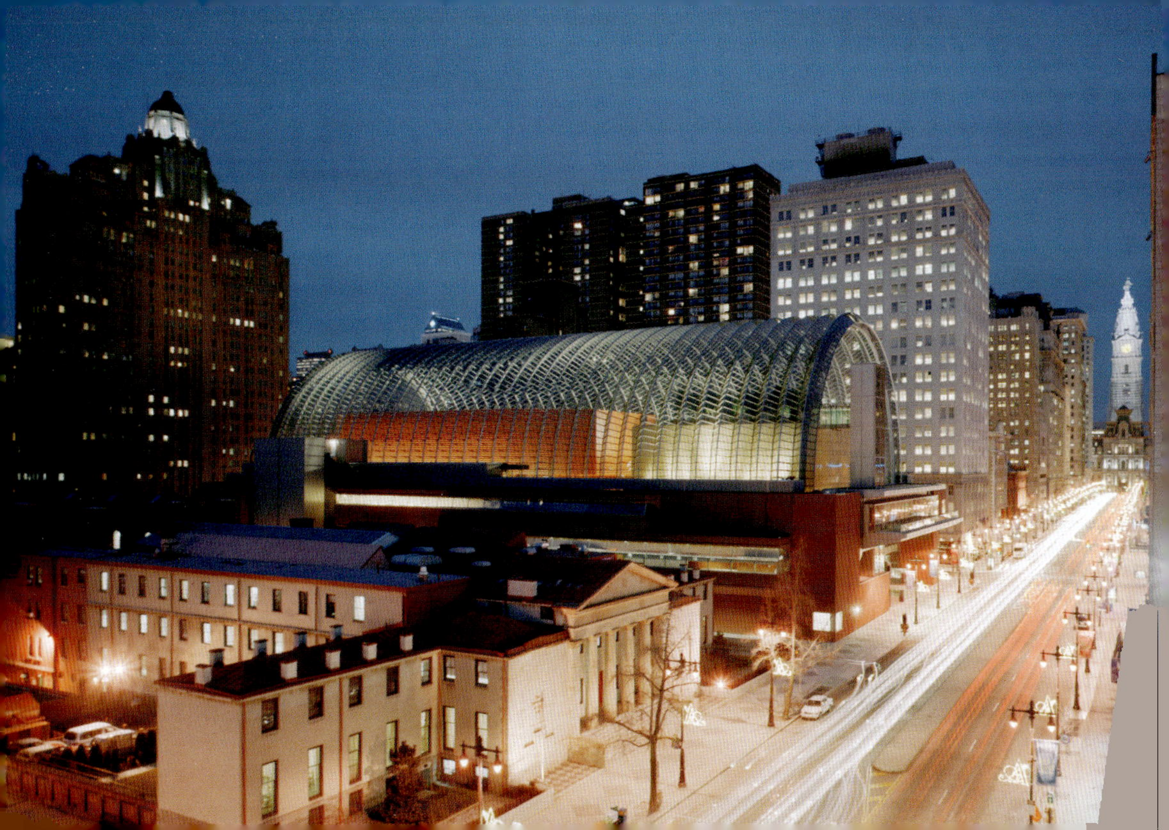

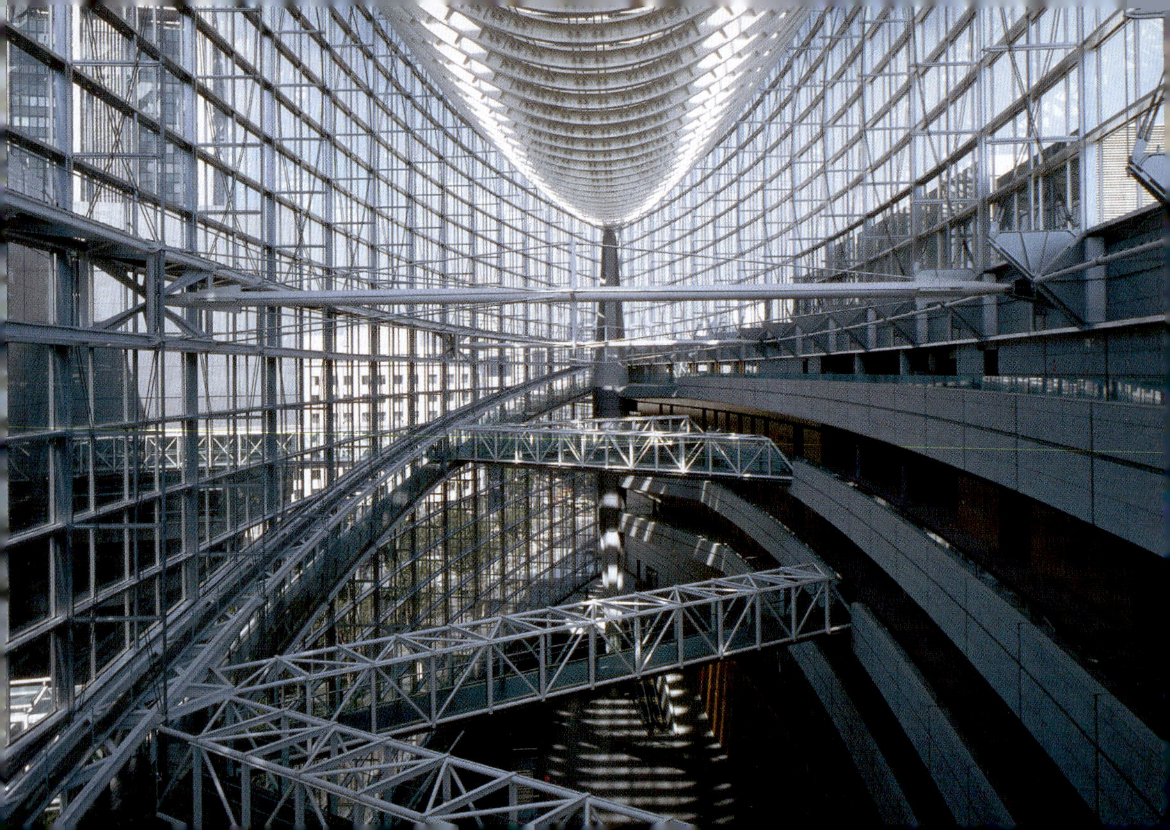

The Challenge

The Cleveland Museum of Art presented an intriguing puzzle. To the south was the lovely Olmsted-designed Fine Arts Garden around Wade Lagoon; on the eastern face, Beaux Arts marble collided with Breuer granite stripes; the northern entrance was marked by Breuer's elemental concrete canopy reaching toward Wade Oval; and the western edge featured service facilities and outbuildings and a hillside descending steeply to Doan Brook. Since the completion of the Breuer addition in 1971, three architectural styles had made up the space: early 1900s Neoclassicism, the midcentury International style, and the elemental late modernism of Breuer's granite stripes. The 1983 library addition on the western side by Dalton, Van Dijk, Johnson and Partners tied in with the more subdued 1958 style.

Meanwhile, transportation had evolved over the decades, and visitors who had once walked to the museum from nearby neighborhoods or trolley stops now arrived in cars. Because the museum's parking lots were tucked away behind the building to the north, visitors entered from that side through what was originally understood as the back door and an entrance to the education and program departments—rather than experiencing the inspiring ascent of the grand south steps into the rotunda flanked by arms and armor and old master paintings. Was it possible to reimagine the museum complex to its best advantage, both logically and aesthetically?

↓ A 2001 aerial view of the museum complex before renovation and construction.

← Viñoly's Tokyo International Forum.

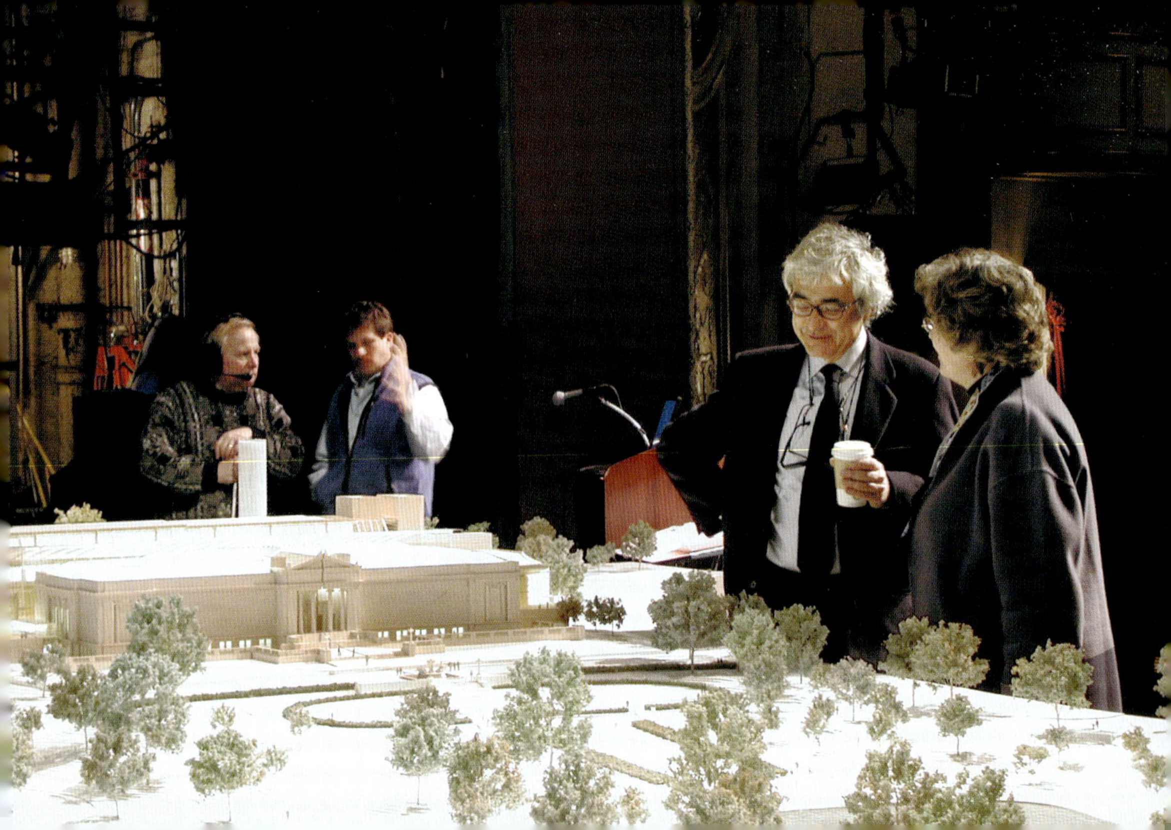

Inviting Public Process

As the planning got under way, the museum organized a series of public events designed to draw insight from interested citizens. In 2002, Lillian Kuri, then director of the nonprofit group Cleveland Public Art, organized one of those events, a public forum with Viñoly at the Ohio Theatre in Cleveland's Playhouse Square. "I think a public process is a statement to the community that you care what they think," she said at the time. "Here, it's also a statement about how beloved this museum is. People genuinely love and care about the institution and they're eager to contribute. Public process makes that bond even stronger."

The strength of the bond that already existed between the museum and the community did not escape Viñoly's notice, either. "The place is so alive. You definitely get the sense that this is not a touristic attraction. It's a resource for the people, part of the life of the city. The most important part of the process of talking to people is that you get a much more realistic idea of what the issues are. For example, you read on paper that there is love for the 1916 building. But when you talk to people you find out that it is not only about being fond of some nice architecture, but that this has become a symbol of what the city feels about itself." To Viñoly, the exercise of public discussion played a vital role. "You explain how your process works, and in doing that you gain a kind of equity. There's nothing like discussion to sort things out. Sometimes all you do is pose unresolvable questions, but then everybody knows the issue has been considered and that a choice has to be made."

← Architect Rafael Viñoly and Katharine Lee Reid (director 2000–2005) chat before a February 2002 forum at the Ohio Theatre in Cleveland's Playhouse Square.

↑ Guests view the building project scale model at a museum donor event.

↑ Marcel Breuer's concrete canopy.

→ Viñoly's "Jewel in the Ring": the original 1916 museum building.

Kuri was impressed. "The amazing thing to me is that this is happening early enough that the museum and the architect can really respond. I've really never met an architect who is so willing and eager to hear broad public input."

Cleveland Quality

One of the messages Viñoly heard loud and clear was that the community treasured its museum and appreciated its quality. "Ultimately, it has to do with what you start with," he said, "which is what is so special about this project, because you start with such extraordinary quality. I am of the position that the public always knows what quality is. It's important in terms of audience, because when the only thing you concentrate on is public relations and image, then eventually it falls apart. You can't sustain something for very long if it isn't very good. That idea drives this process: the need to let the quality of the art make the best first impression. It all exists just to help people connect with art. It's almost unbelievable, the kind of quality you have in this place—very much in

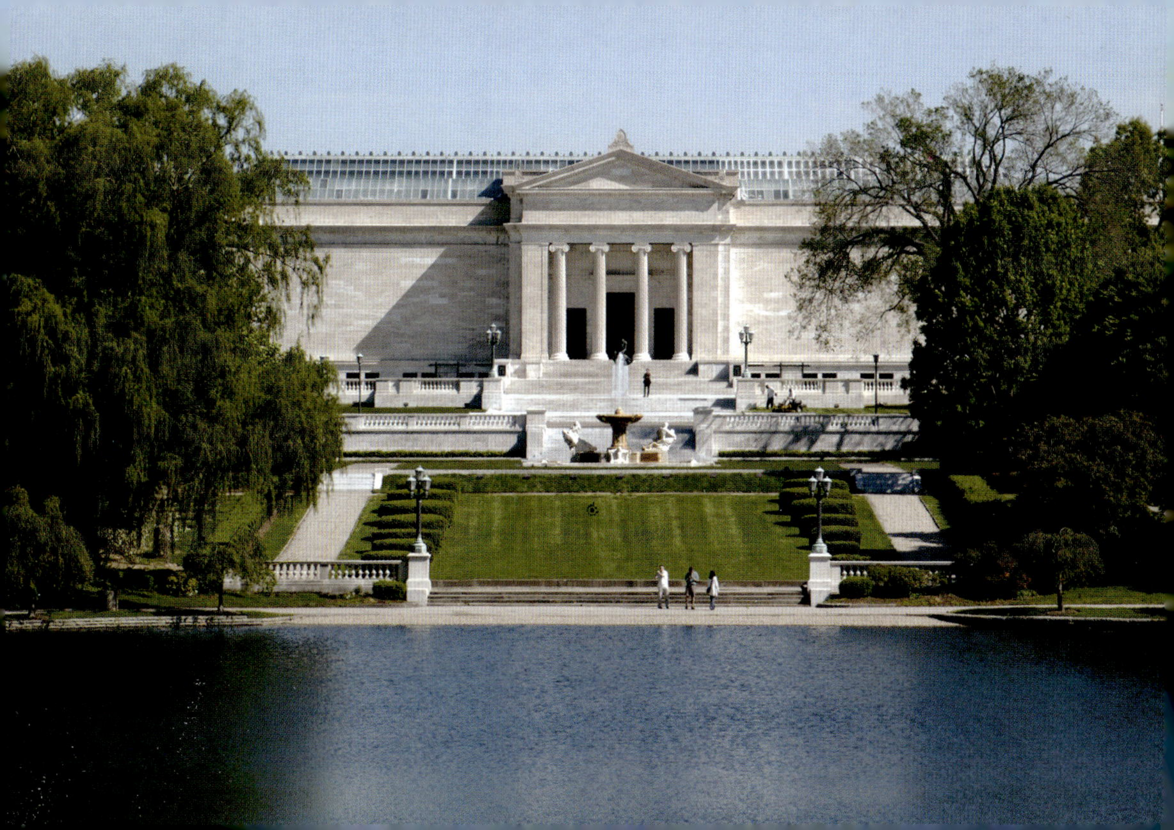

↑ Viñoly's conceptual sketch: original museum building at the top, Breuer building at the bottom (below).

→ Site plan with proposed new construction superimposed.

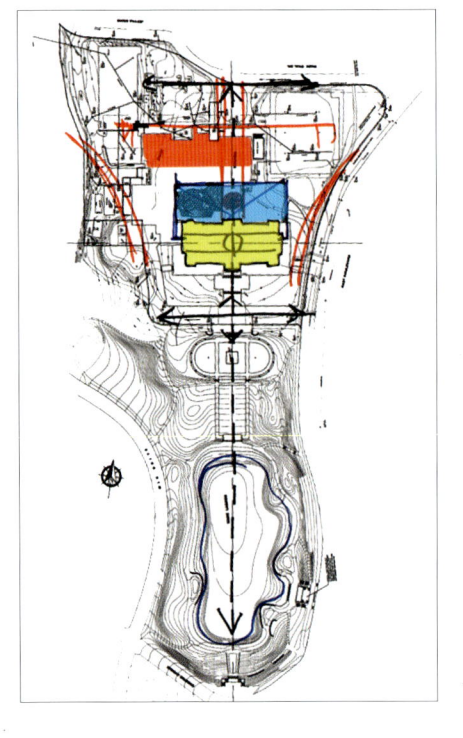

Viñoly site sketch showing indoor/outdoor circulation concept. →

parallel with the orchestra. How is it that you have such an orchestra here? How did you get an art museum this good? These are the kinds of things that are the sustainers of urban life. They lend support to how you present your city, and they can convince people to be part of this vibrant place."

The Jewel in the Ring

The 1916 building is what the architect describes as "the jewel in the ring setting" of the design. The 1971 Breuer building on the northern side of the complex is celebrated also, as a powerful distillation of the late modernist aesthetic, a dramatic sculptural form in itself. These divergent styles speak metaphorically of the extraordinary diversity of expression within the museum.

Viñoly's plan called for removing the 1958 and 1983 additions and using new construction to create a circulation pattern that expands rather than disrupts the natural flow of the original building. Two wings connect to the east and west of the 1916 building, the exterior walls stepping outward as they sweep north. With spirited

22 / THE CLEVELAND MUSEUM OF ART

THE CLEVELAND MUSEUM OF ART

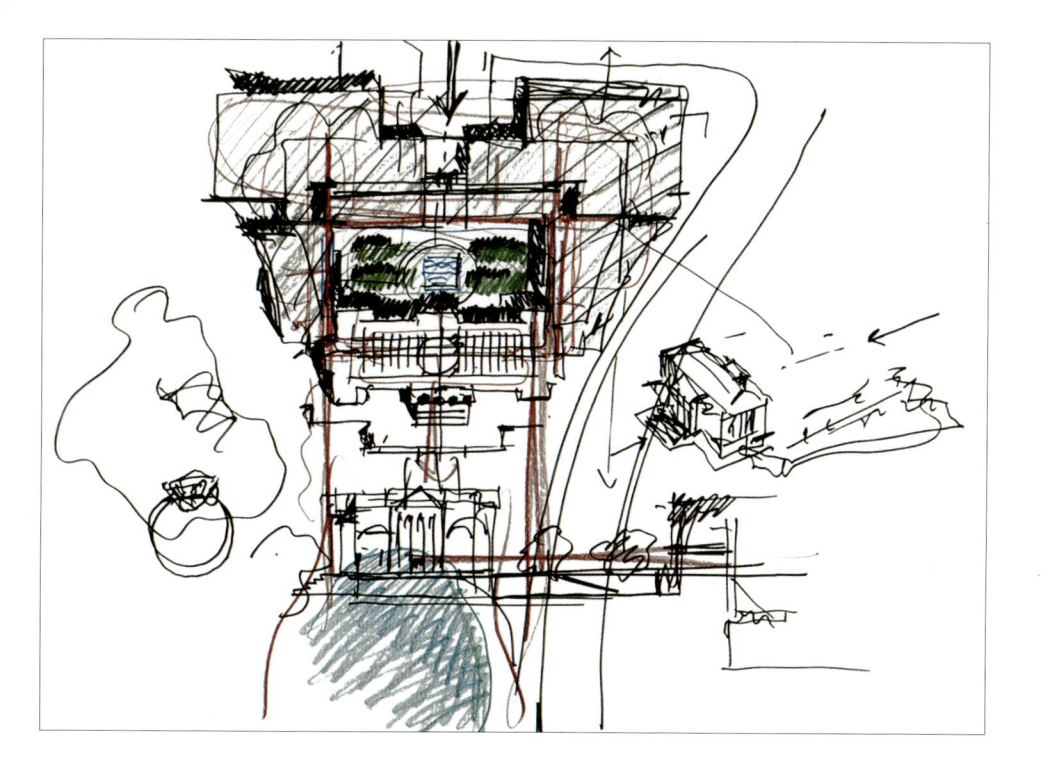

→ Video still showing Viñoly sketching.

→→ Final site plan, 2013.

→→→ Aerial photo, 2011.

visual wit, Viñoly faced these flanking wings with horizontal bands of light and dark stone that begin on the north by matching up with Breuer's granite stripes. They incrementally shift to wider bands of light and fewer of dark as the walls get closer to the white marble of the original building. The actual connections to the 1916 building are all glass—creating a visual impression that the new and old are connected by light and air, not by stone and steel. At the center, an expansive glass roof arches to the north from the old building, enclosing a grand new atrium; farther to the north the Breuer building remains, rededicated to its original purpose as a

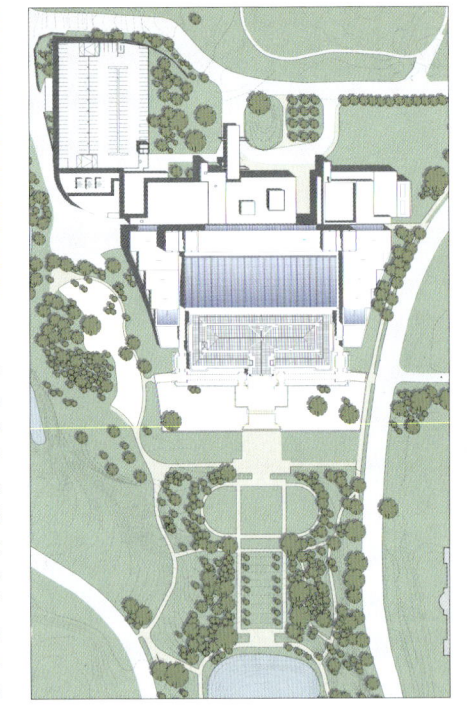

24 / THE CLEVELAND MUSEUM OF ART

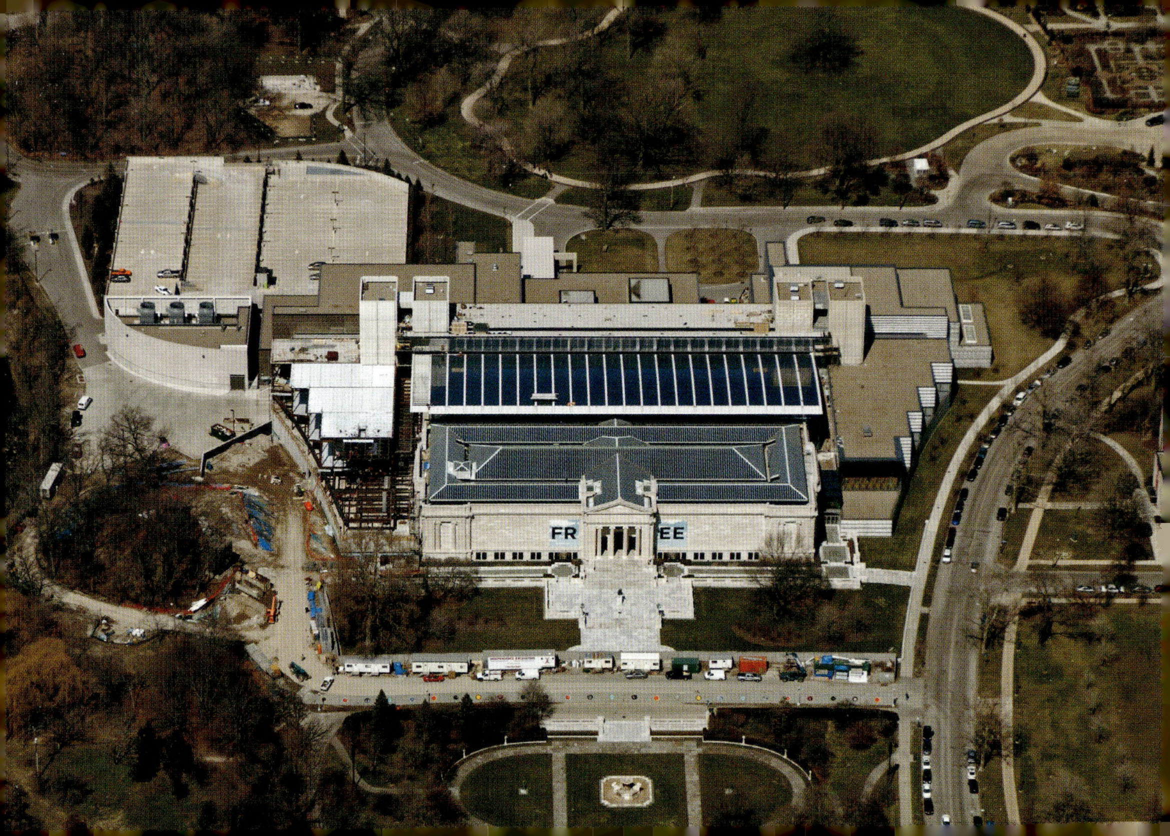
FR
EE

Level one

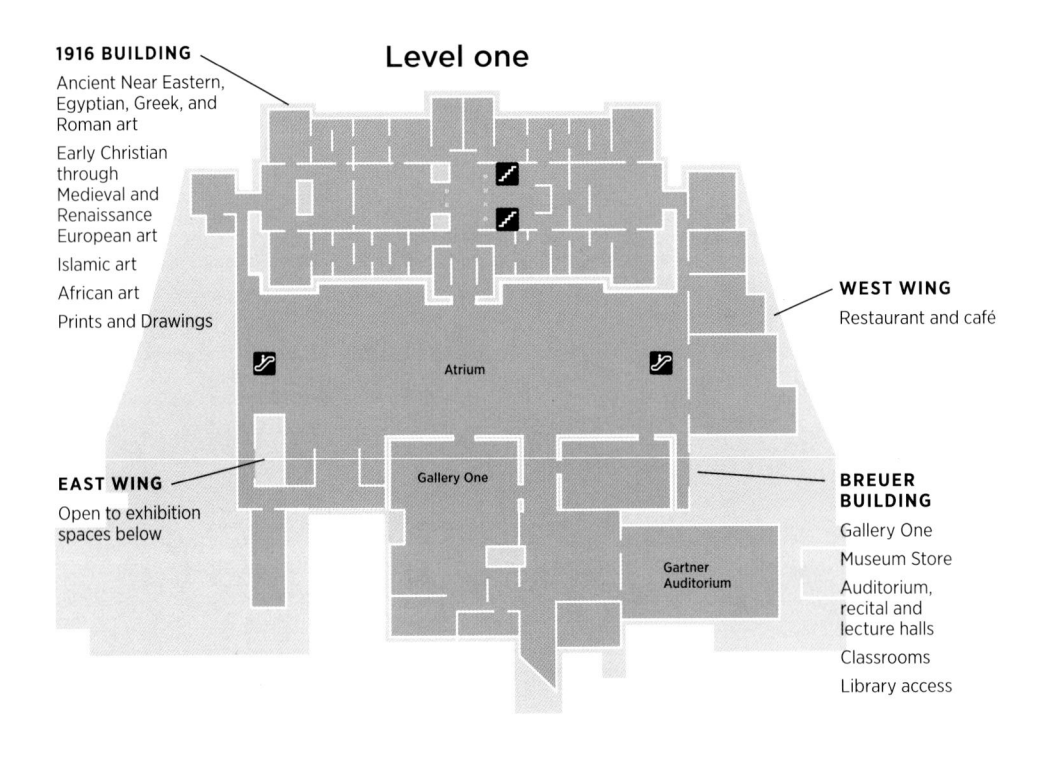

1916 BUILDING
Ancient Near Eastern, Egyptian, Greek, and Roman art
Early Christian through Medieval and Renaissance European art
Islamic art
African art
Prints and Drawings

WEST WING
Restaurant and café

EAST WING
Open to exhibition spaces below

BREUER BUILDING
Gallery One
Museum Store
Auditorium, recital and lecture halls
Classrooms
Library access

Atrium
Gallery One
Gartner Auditorium

Level two

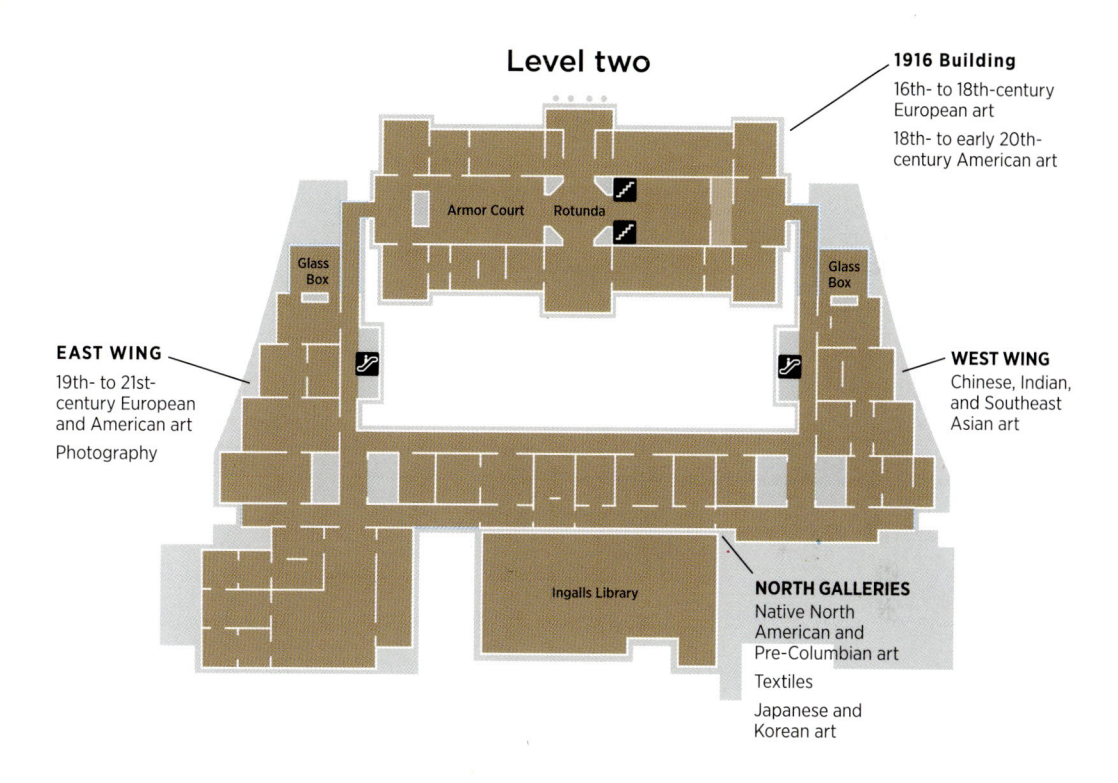

1916 Building
16th- to 18th-century European art

18th- to early 20th-century American art

Armor Court

Rotunda

Glass Box

Glass Box

EAST WING
19th- to 21st-century European and American art

Photography

WEST WING
Chinese, Indian, and Southeast Asian art

Ingalls Library

NORTH GALLERIES
Native North American and Pre-Columbian art

Textiles

Japanese and Korean art

THE CLEVELAND MUSEUM OF ART / 27

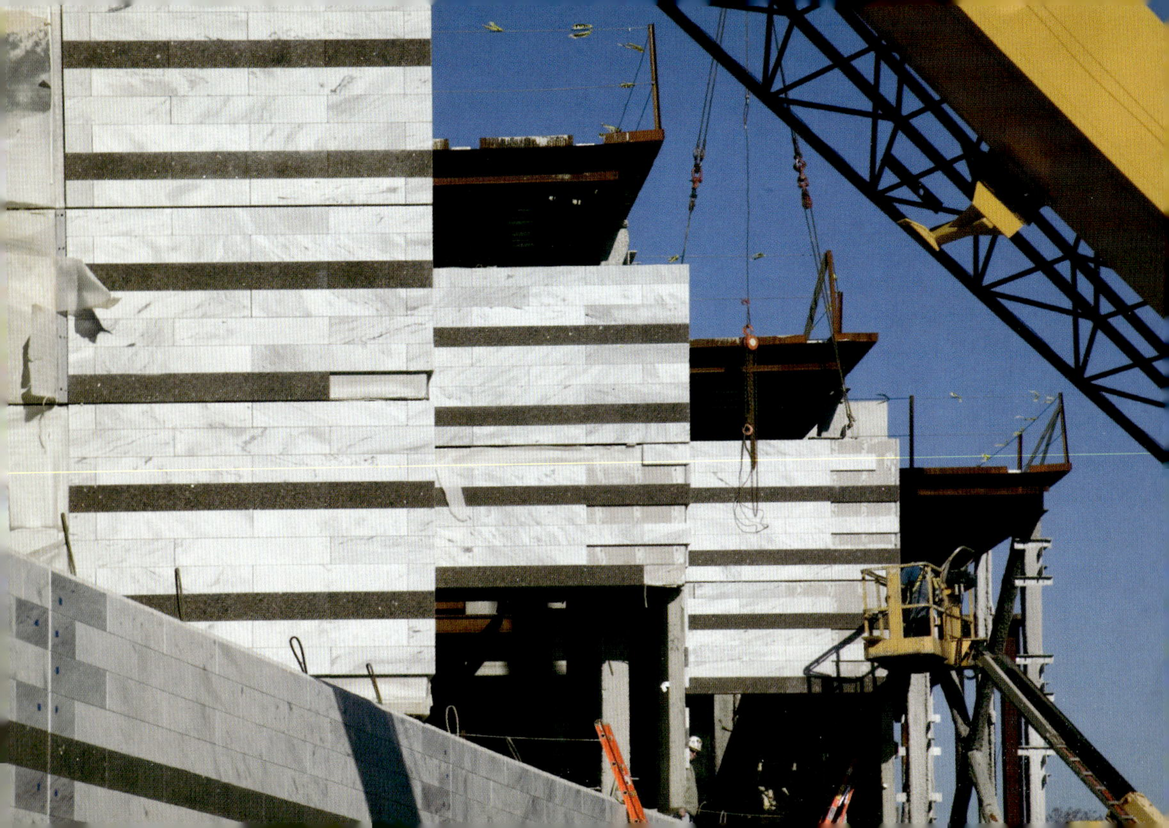

Transformation

comprehensive education facility. Northwest of that is an expanded parking garage, largely underground. The original 1916 building is completely restored, including the return of all the original skylights.

The museum's curators recognized right away that the project presented an almost unheard-of opportunity: to reinstall the entire collection of one of the world's great art museums, all at once. Not only could the museum look back at 40,000 acquisitions over the preceding nine decades and reevaluate the organization and presentation of the collection, but the gallery installations themselves could all follow to a single, comprehensive design scheme. Thus began a solid decade of work shaping the evolving architectural plan to accommodate all facets of the collection, with the goal of creating an optimal experience of art in space.

The project dramatically transforms the museum experience. Most visitors park in the garage and emerge from the north into the bright atrium. This space serves as the central point of orientation and a kind of "commons" for the museum. From that central point, nearly every key element of the museum experience is visible by direct sight lines. Straight ahead is the first level of the 1916 building with prints and drawings galleries just inside the doors, and farther on are the collections of ancient,

↓ Museum officials and guests join in a groundbreaking ceremony to initiate the project.

← East wing under construction.

→ De-installing the galleries in 2005: Asian sculpture.

↠ Art handlers move an ancient Persian winged genie.

↠ Gartner Auditorium after renovation.

African, Byzantine, medieval, and Renaissance art. The center of the north-facing stone facade of that building, which was covered up by the 1950s museum addition, has been restored to evoke its original state. More than one visitor has commented that, framed under the atrium glass, the marble north facade itself is a work of art.

To the left and up one level is the east wing, with its modern and contemporary art and works from Europe and America since the nineteenth century. Below those galleries are two special exhibition spaces on the lower level. To the right is the west wing, with the Asian galleries on the second level and the museum store, café, and restaurant on the atrium level.

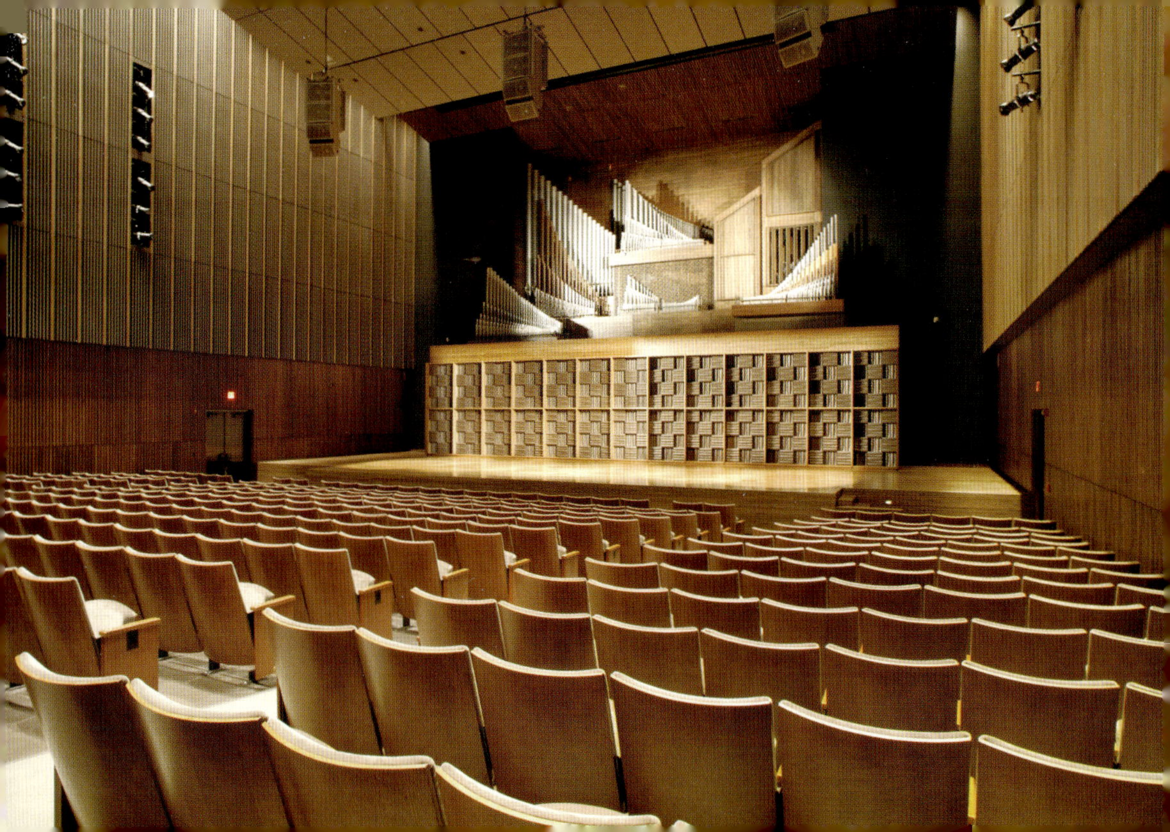

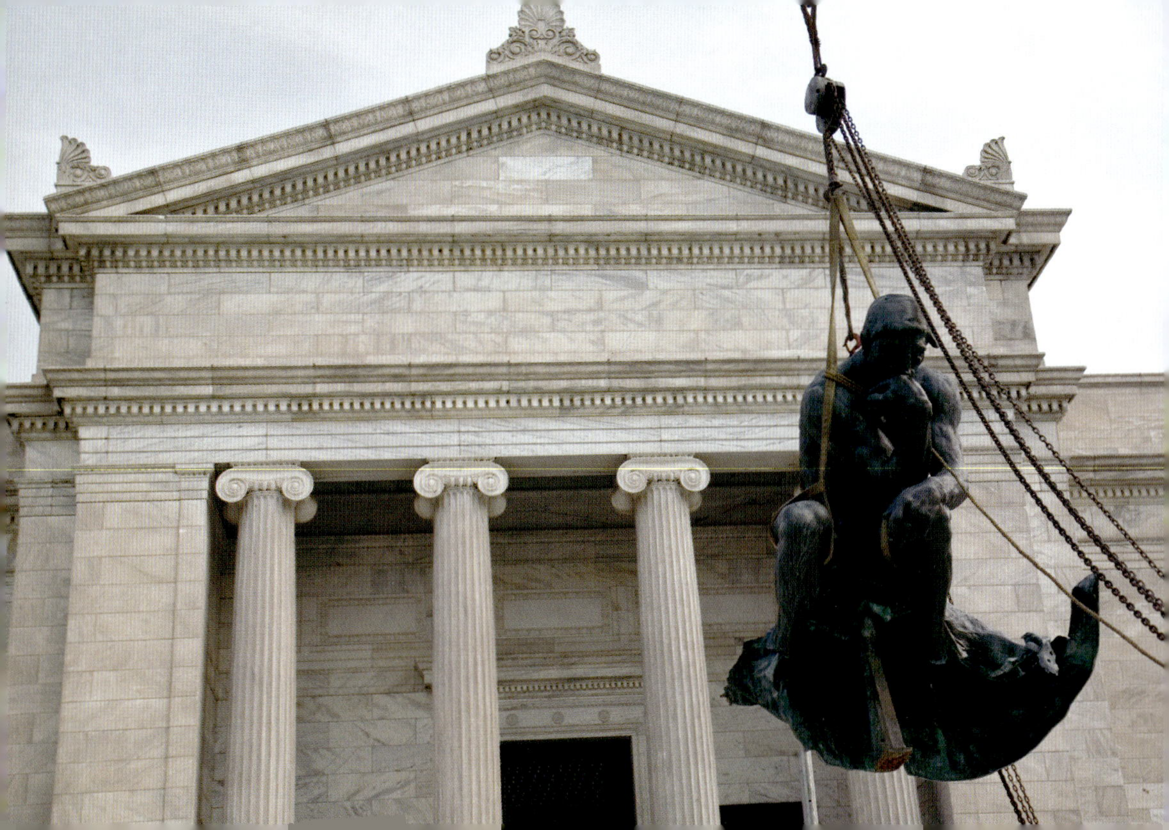

← Each work of art is tagged for storage: Antonello Gaggini marble of Saint Margaret in the foreground and Filippino Lippi Holy Family tondo in the background.

← De-installing the galleries in 2005: French nineteenth-century painting.

← Auguste Rodin's *The Thinker* moved during construction.

↑ Timothy Rub (director 2006–2009) and trustee Ellen Stirn Mavec stand in the 1916 galleries during reinstallation.

↗ Reinstalling the collection offered the opportunity to examine and treat many works of art in the new conservation labs.

→ Curator of ancient art Michael Bennett (left) reviews a gallery model at the offices of local architects Collins Gordon Bostwick.

34 / THE CLEVELAND MUSEUM OF ART

Behind and above are the north galleries, with the Japanese and Korean collections, textiles, and the art of the Americas. At ground level just to the east of the passage from the north lobby and the atrium is Gallery One. This innovative learning center combines real works of art with interactive features designed to help visitors of all ages connect with the collection. A prominent corner of that space, with windows on the atrium, is a focus gallery for exhibitions built around a single work of art. An extension of the Gallery One technology allows visitors to roam throughout the museum using small hand-held devices that connect wirelessly to Gallery One's vast wealth of interpretive material; no built-in interactive features or video monitors clutter the gallery spaces. Strategically placed glass entry doors allow a person standing in the atrium to look right into the galleries and see works of art characteristic of the collections in those spaces—for example, an ancient bronze Apollo straight ahead, Claude Monet's *Water Lilies (Agapanthus)* to the east, or monumental southeast Asian sculptures to the west—and thus to know without reading a sign or asking a question what art is where.

← The Gallery One collections wall allows families to explore the entire collection virtually.

↓ Rodin's *The Age of Bronze* greeted visitors when the east wing glass box first opened.

THE CLEVELAND MUSEUM OF ART / 35

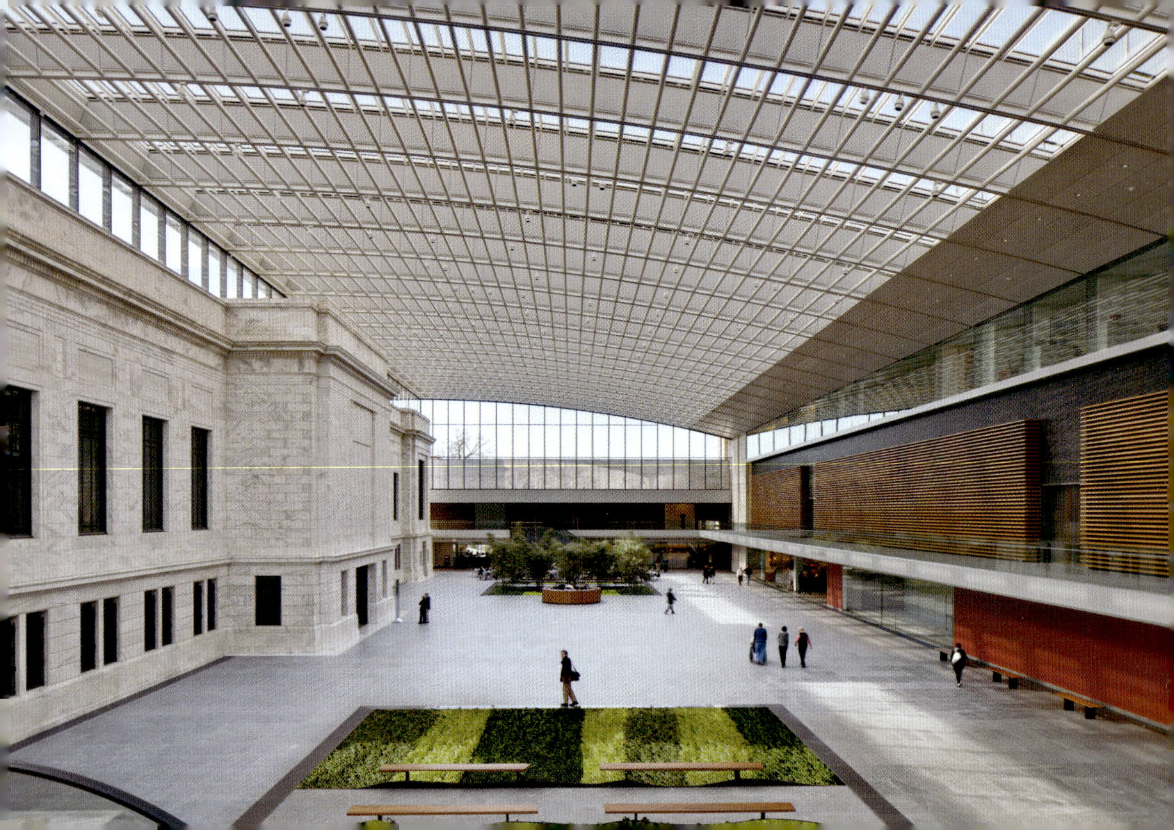

Make Your Own Path

While sustaining the unbroken timeline of art history, the scheme also creates mini-museums within the larger structure. For example, the 1916 building becomes a comprehensive presentation of European art from the Middle Ages through the early twentieth century, while the west wing serves as a museum of Asia, and a museum of the Americas resides in the north galleries. Visitors can walk from gallery to gallery, following chronology—but because each wing is flanked by an allée along the edge of the atrium, it is also possible to enter and exit galleries in numerous places without being forced to follow a single pathway from one gallery to the next. The concept provides visitors greater ease of navigation as well as the flexibility to control their experience. The architect's earliest plans did not include an allée along the northern edge of the atrium; the addition of that key feature is a testament to Viñoly's willingness to listen to public feedback, and to the museum's drive to make the reimagined museum all that it could be.

The $350 million project increases the museum's floor space by about 43 percent, with 38,000 additional net square feet of gallery and exhibition space, 32,000

A system of allées flanking the atrium makes it possible to choose whether to experience the galleries in sequence, or according to your own preferences.

← Rafeal Viñoly's breathtaking atrium.

THE CLEVELAND MUSEUM OF ART / **37**

→ Escalators adjacent to the new east wing.

feet of convening space (primarily the atrium and other gathering places), and 8,500 square feet dedicated to the Gallery One learning center. While the total increase in space is significant, its configuration is just as important. The renowned Asian collection, which for decades resided in a dark labyrinth of galleries, now has a fresh space of its own on the main gallery level. Ingalls Library, moved to the upper two floors of the Breuer building, is now open to the public and features a bright, sky-lit reading room. Gartner Auditorium received a complete renovation to turn it into a more versatile and balanced acoustic environment, honoring Breuer's original design with a brighter visual sense. A number of new and renovated special exhibition spaces of different shapes and sizes allow the museum to bring a greater variety of exciting exhibitions to Cleveland. The café area at the western end of the atrium offers pleasant casual seating while the adjoining restaurant overlooks the surrounding park.

Light and Space

The atrium presents the museum as an experience of light and open space, of long vistas that connect points of interest. Indeed, a desire for natural light in the museum was frequently expressed during the planning stages, not only for its aesthetic qualities, but for the aid in navigation that sight lines to external reference points can provide. Although many works of art are very sensitive to light, the sun does no harm to objects such as bronze or stone sculptures, which are displayed to their best advantage in such a setting. The gallery spaces are

↑ Light beckons visitors into the atrium from the north entrance.

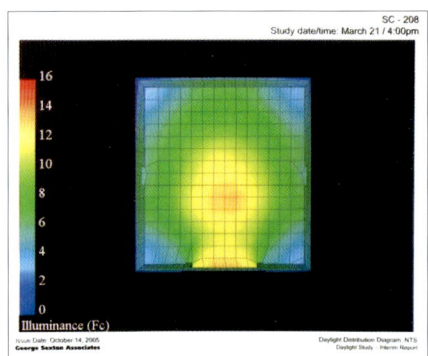

configured to allow natural light to illuminate certain areas designed for works that enjoy the sun.

An overall analysis of light in the galleries was carried out by George Sexton Associates. "The visitor's experience," says Sexton, "is shaped not only by the absolute levels of brightness, but also by the change in brightness that is perceived while moving through the museum. We are reducing the overall amount of daylight that makes it to the gallery walls in order to meet the museum's conservation standards. Despite

← Glass on stone: the new and old buildings connect very lightly.

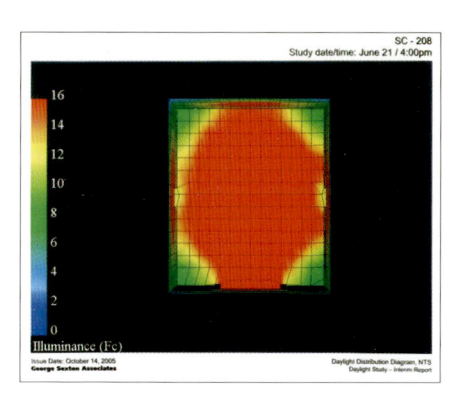

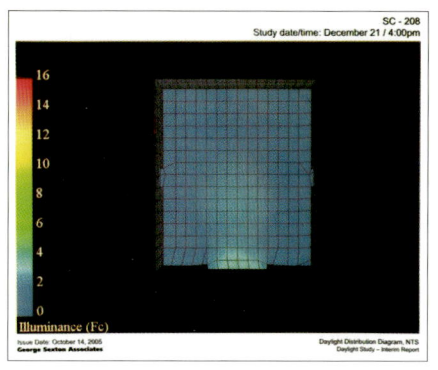

← George Sexton Associates daylight studies in 2005 showing the Neoclassical gallery in the 1916 building at 4:00 p.m. on March 21, June 21, and December 21.

← View to the south out the east wing glass box and allée, 2012 (Martin Creed's balloon installation, *Work No. 965: Half the air in a given space*, on left).

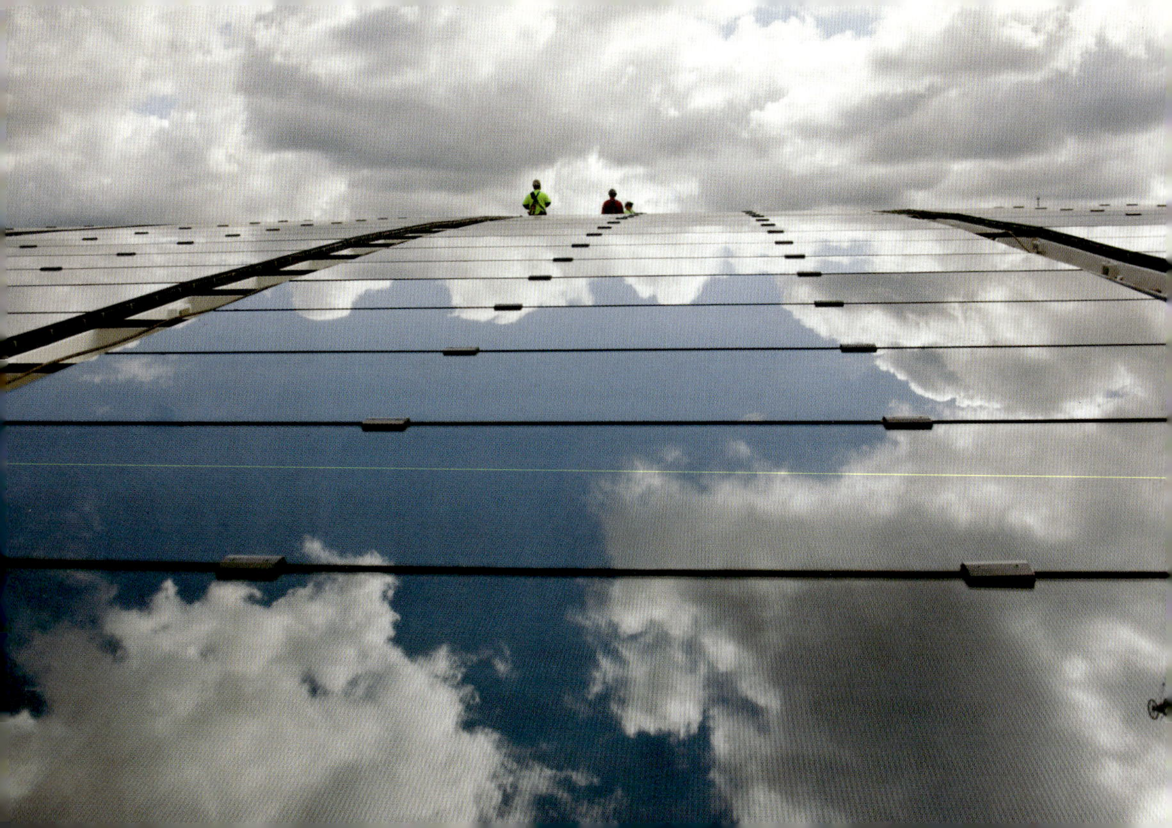

these decreased levels, though, the visitor will have an impression of more light. Some of this has been achieved by restoring the experience of the original building design—for example, by opening up skylights and lay lights around the rotunda that had been blocked off by later construction. But a lot of it has to do with paying special attention to areas of transition. As you move from one space to another, we want to make sure there are no dramatic leaps in brightness."

Hurdles

The considerable complexities of completing a facilities master plan and a comprehensive renovation and expansion project were exacerbated in Cleveland at many turns. First, museum director Robert P. Bergman, initiator of the facilities plan, died tragically and unexpectedly in 1999 just as the process got under way. The "dot-com bust" of 1999–2000 caused a temporary drop in investment funds. The September 11, 2001, tragedy occurred on the very day the project architect was announced, and the subsequent recession slowed fundraising efforts.

↑ Atrium under construction.

← Installing atrium glass.

↑ Atrium at dusk: museum store at left, café tables at right.

→ Steven Kestner, president of the board of trustees, director David Franklin, and former board president Alfred Rankin stand near Caravaggio's *Crucifixion of St. Andrew* (left to right).

Katharine Lee Reid, Sherman Lee's daughter, had been appointed director in 2000 and led the museum through the initial pre-construction stages of the project before she retired in 2005. The next director, Timothy Rub, who had grown up visiting the Philadelphia Museum of Art, departed after only three years because the untimely death of Philadelphia's director Anne d'Harnoncourt created an unexpected opening for the directorship of what he considered his "hometown" museum. The worldwide economic crash of 2008–2009 necessitated a temporary halt to all construction, and a longer timetable was instituted to allow the board of trustees to vote at incremental points to approve funding for each stage. Despite these significant hurdles, the museum persevered and was able to present a project whose final phase was already well under way when director David Franklin began his tenure in 2010. Credit goes to the determined museum staff and the steady leadership of the board of trustees building committee, co-chaired during the 2000s by James Bartlett and Michael Horvitz. Some fifteen years after planning began in earnest, the transformation of the Cleveland Museum of Art was complete.

44 / THE CLEVELAND MUSEUM OF ART

Installations of the Collection

1916 Building, Level One

These galleries begin with art from the area that gave rise to the oldest cities on earth—the region stretching from present-day Iraq north to the Black Sea—and follow the growth of civilization and the evolution of art through ancient Egypt, classical Greece and Rome, into the early Christian and medieval world and Africa. Cleveland's collections of ancient art are not nearly the largest. The British Museum in London, the Musée du Louvre in Paris, the Metropolitan Museum of Art in New York, and the Museum of Fine Arts, Boston, built enormous collections of antiquities thanks to avid nineteenth-century collectors whose Grand Tours often yielded literal boatloads of artifacts. Cleveland's holdings, in contrast, were built one object at a time, acquired by astute curators and discerning directors. Cleveland's collection presents a selection of masterworks rather than an exhaustive survey of the ancient world.

The galleries are organized thematically rather than by strict chronology. Entering the galleries by turning left after coming in from the atrium, visitors first encounter art from Asia Minor and the Fertile Crescent,

↑ The atrium in the evening, entrance to 1916 level one galleries in the center of the building.

THE CLEVELAND MUSEUM OF ART / 45

including small, portable objects that exemplify the art of migratory societies, such as the 3000 BC *Stargazer* from Anatolia.

From here the progression moves from Greece to Rome by way of Etruscan and South Italian art that predated the Greek influence on the Italian peninsula. Early Christian and Byzantine art follows, and a circuit of the galleries around the perimeter culminates in a dramatic room devoted to the eleventh-century Guelph Treasure and related works of medieval Europe. At the center is a room called "The Gift of the River"—home to the Egyptian collection that inspired the great 1992 exhibition *Egypt's Dazzling Sun: Amenhotep III and His World*. The museum's collection of African art, most of it much more recent, is for the first time installed adjacent to the collections of Egyptian art, unifying these works produced on the African continent.

Displaying 1,700 largely three-dimensional objects required fabricating well over one thousand mounts, each designed to hold works of art in a way that is both extremely secure and unobtrusive enough to show off each work's great qualities. The gallery and lighting designers made sure each room would bring out the best in the works on view there—sometimes incorporating arched doorways and other elements to evoke a particular setting, other times creating more neutral spaces.

A central lobby divides this level where the scope of the contents of the adjoining galleries is suggested by two striking masterworks installed at the base of the stairs from the rotunda above: the bronze statue *Apollo the Python-Slayer,* attributed to Praxiteles and probably made between 400 and 330 BC, and the large painted wood *Crucifix with Scenes of the Passion*, made in Pisa in the early thirteenth century. Both are visible through glass doors from the atrium.

Crossing that lobby from the Guelph Treasure into the western half of level one, visitors first encounter galleries of high and international Gothic art, including manuscripts, the unique early fourteenth-century French *Table Fountain*, and *Three Mourners* from the tomb of the Burgundian duke Philip the Bold. The next gallery displays Italian Gothic art including the remarkable altarpiece *Virgin and Child with Saints*, made in Siena

← A school group visits the ancient Egyptian galleries.

↑ Tomb mourners from the court of Burgundy in the medieval galleries.

THE CLEVELAND MUSEUM OF ART / 47

→ Rotations of manuscripts are displayed in the context of other medieval and Renaissance art.

→ The famed Chaumont tapestries fill the walls in a gallery of manuscripts and textiles.

African art on level one of the 1916 building. →

around 1300. French and English stained glass follow in the next room, leading into Spanish Gothic art.

The southwest corner features late Gothic art from German and Austria, with highlights including a pair of sculptures by Tilman Riemenschneider representing Saints Stephen and Lawrence. The next room features Netherlandish art. French textiles and manuscripts occupy the gallery in the northwest corner, with the famed floor-to-ceiling Chaumont Tapestries.

Continuing clockwise, sixteenth-century German paintings are followed by installations of Islamic textiles. In the center are three large galleries of Italian art of the fourteenth through sixteenth centuries, with key works including the large Filippino Lippi tondo *The Holy Family with Saint John the Baptist and Saint Margaret*, the small Valerio Belli pendant *Mars, Minerva, Venus, and Cupid*, and the panoramic *Race of the Palio in the Streets of Florence* by Giovanni Toscani, depicting a horse race traditionally held on the feast of John the Baptist. From the central lobby, a symmetrical pair of monumental marble stairs ascends to the second level, emerging at the western edge of the rotunda.

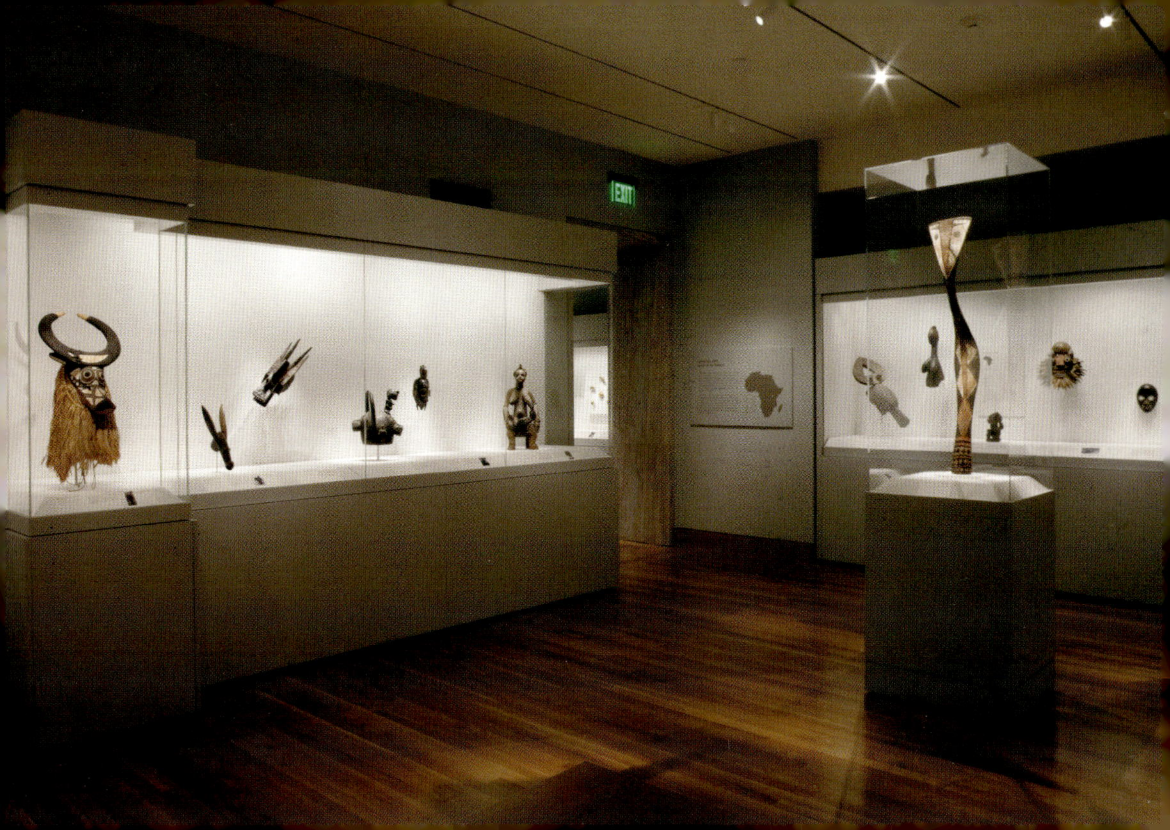
EXIT

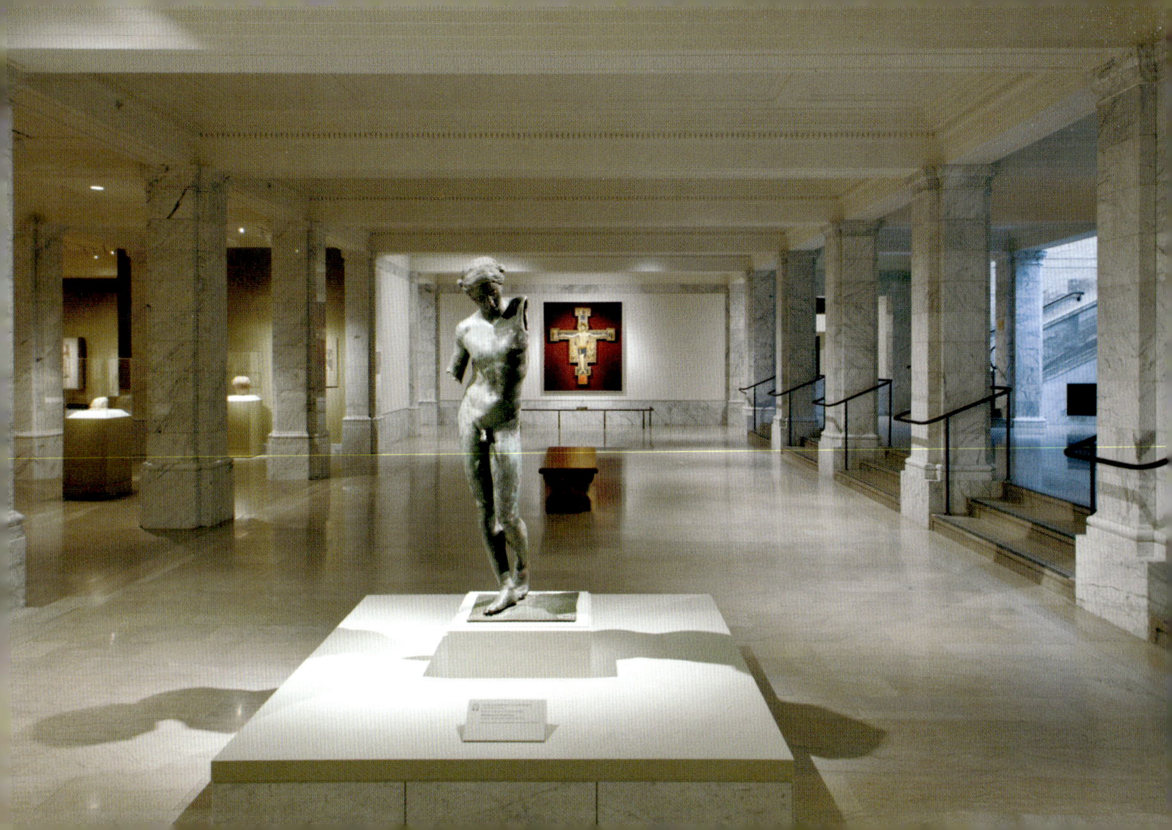

The upper-floor galleries of the 1916 building contain the heart of the museum's collection of European art as well as the formative stages in the development of American art. The perimeter galleries are arranged around a suite of three large spaces: the Armor Court, the rotunda, and a barrel-vaulted gallery of Italian painting and sculpture of the seventeenth and eighteenth centuries including masterworks by Caravaggio and Guido Reni (with a balcony serving as an intimate space for the display of miniatures and other small works from seventeenth-century Europe). The rotunda, presided over by Antonio Canova's marble *Terpsichore Lyran,* is the central spot from which to explore the building.

Just inside the south entrance are cases displaying the art of Fabergé on the left and American decorative art, including the work of Louis Comfort Tiffany, on the right. A turn to the left leads into the Reinberger Gallery and starts the visit with an impressive group of masterworks—in this one room are famous pieces including Nicolas Poussin's *Holy Family on the Steps*, El Greco's *Christ on the Cross*, Diego Velázquez's *Jester Calabazas*, Francisco de Zurbarán's *Christ and the Virgin in the House at Nazareth*, Peter Paul Rubens's *Portrait of Isabella Brant*, and Sir Anthony van Dyck's *Portrait of a Woman and Child*. Next comes Dutch baroque art, including landscapes, genre paintings, still lifes, and portraits, among them a stunning oil by Frans Hals, *Tieleman Roosterman*. The following three rooms feature European sculpture, decorative art, and painting from the seventeenth and eighteenth centuries.

French and German art from the eighteenth cen-

← Bronze Apollo attributed to Praxiteles and monumental Pisan cross, level one lobby of 1916 building with double stair to level two at right.

↑ A drawing class surrounds Antonio Canova's *Terpsichore Lyran.*

→ The Armor Court and rotunda, 2012.

↠ The Baroque Court seen from the balcony looking toward the central rotunda.

tury, including paintings by Jean Siméon Chardin and Jean-Honoré Fragonard and rococo decorative art and furniture, graces the next room, which opens to a vaulted gallery of Neoclassical painting and sculpture with Jacques-Louis David's great *Cupid and Psyche* and a suite of five monumental paintings by Charles Meynier. Adjacent is a gallery of French Neoclassical decorative art.

British art of the eighteenth and nineteenth centuries continues the clockwise tour in a room featuring J. M. W. Turner's *Burning of the Houses of Lords and Commons* and works by Sir Thomas Lawrence, Thomas Gainsborough, John Constable, and Sir Joshua Reynolds. The jump to the New World begins with a small space devoted to silver and ceramics from London and colonial America as well as porcelain and pottery from England's greatest manufactories.

In the next room, displays of colonial American portraiture and decorative art include canvases by John Singleton Copley, Gilbert Stuart, and Benjamin West, as well as fine examples of furniture and silver by Jacob Hurd and others. American art from the Federal period is

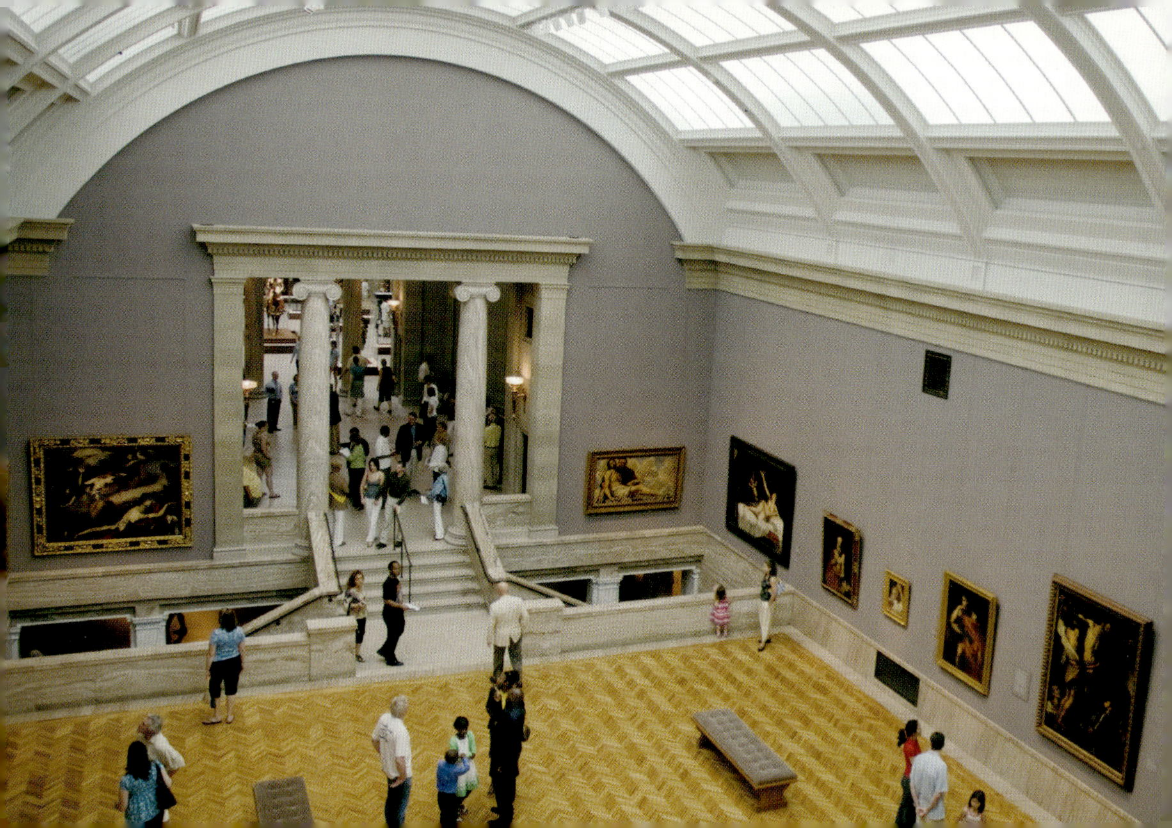

→ Janet Cardiff's sound installation *Forty-Part Motet* in the Baroque Court, 2013.

→→ Cellist Matthew Allen from the Cleveland Institute of Music plays in the Reinberger Gallery with masterworks by Peter Paul Rubens, Nicolas Poussin, Sir Anthony van Dyck, Francisco de Goya, El Greco, Francisco de Zurbarán, and others.

next (along with a passage to the east allée), followed by a spectacular room of landscape paintings from the mid-nineteenth century, with masterpieces by Thomas Cole and Albert Bierstadt as well as Frederic Edwin Church's *Twilight in the Wilderness*. The following gallery celebrates more icons of American art, with Winslow Homer's *Brierwood Pipe*, Thomas Eakins's *Biglin Brothers Turning the Stake*, and William Sidney Mount's *Power of Music*. Concluding the circuit is a large gallery featuring elegant paintings by John Singer Sargent and William Merritt Chase, exemplars of America's Gilded Age, juxtaposed with the work of Ashcan School painters typified by George Bellows, whose *Stag at Sharkey's* explores a less glamorous side of American life.

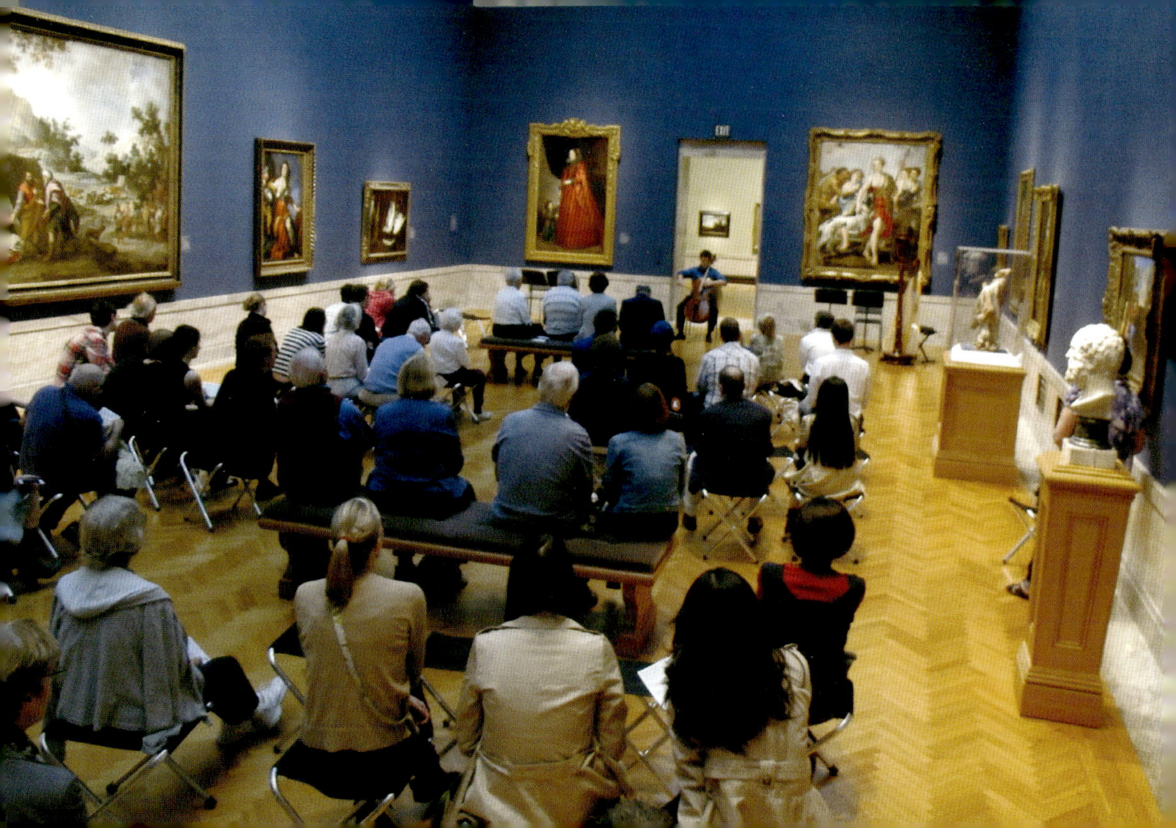
EXIT

↑ Designer, director, and curator discuss the installation of Impressionist art in the new east wing.

→ Visitors browse in the Impressionist galleries of the east wing.

The East Wing

Within the distinctive zigzag exterior footprint, the more than 27,000 square feet of galleries present striking spaces arranged along a perfectly aligned sequence of doorways that establishes a clear sight line all the way from the contemporary collections to the glass cube at the southern end of the addition. One of the stated goals of the expansion project was to create a sense of openness and connection to the neighborhood, and nothing expresses the success of that endeavor more powerfully than when a pedestrian strolling along East Boulevard glances up to marvel at great works of art on view in the glass box gallery. Similarly, the impression from within these rooms is one of connection to the surrounding landscape, as natural light illuminates every space and windows offer a view out to the street.

The collections contained in the east wing include some of the museum's most noted and beloved works of art, picking up the thread of European art where it leaves off in the early 1800s in the 1916 building and continuing that evolution through Impressionism, Post-Impressionism, and modern and contemporary art.

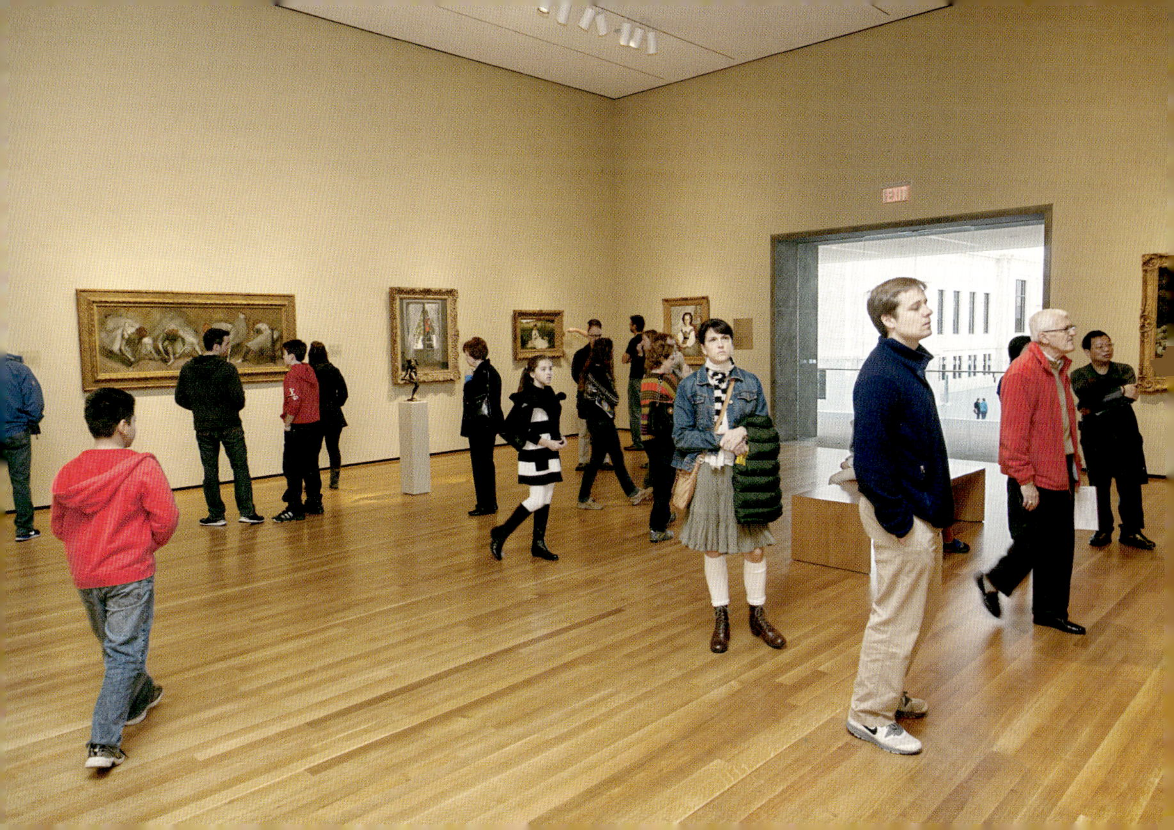
EXIT

↑ Violist Ji Young Nam from the Cleveland Institute of Music plays in the contemporary galleries.

→ Rafael Viñoly's west wing, 2013.

American art also continues, from the early twentieth century and up to the present day, from Cleveland School artists to Andy Warhol and Sol LeWitt. Three separate spaces are devoted to decorative art and design, and three adjoining galleries focus primarily on photography and other light-sensitive materials. The southern end of the east wing allée connects to the 1916 building and galleries of the immediately preceding eras of Western art history.

The West Wing

The stepped west wing footprint mirrors that of the east. The glass box gallery at the southern end—here not overlooking the street, but poised above a sloping wooded hillside and Doan Brook—features bronze and stone sculpture of China and Southeast Asia. As in the east wing, the doorways are aligned to allow a long vista from the glass box all the way to the north end of the wing. The next gallery in that direction features early Indian, Mughal, and Chola art. Many superb works from the museum's renowned Asian collections reside in these spaces, including the sixth-century Cambodian limestone sculpture *Krishna Govardhana*, the eleventh-century Chola bronze *Nataraja, Shiva as the King of Dance*, and the red sandstone *Nagini* from the second century, exemplifying the voluptuous female figures that are frequently depicted in South Indian art. Buddhist sculpture and works from ancient China occupy the next suite of galleries to the north. Highlights include a black lacquer *Bodhisattva* from the ninth-century Tang Dynasty and a Zhou Dynasty lacquered wood drum stand from the fourth or third century BC—ingeniously created in

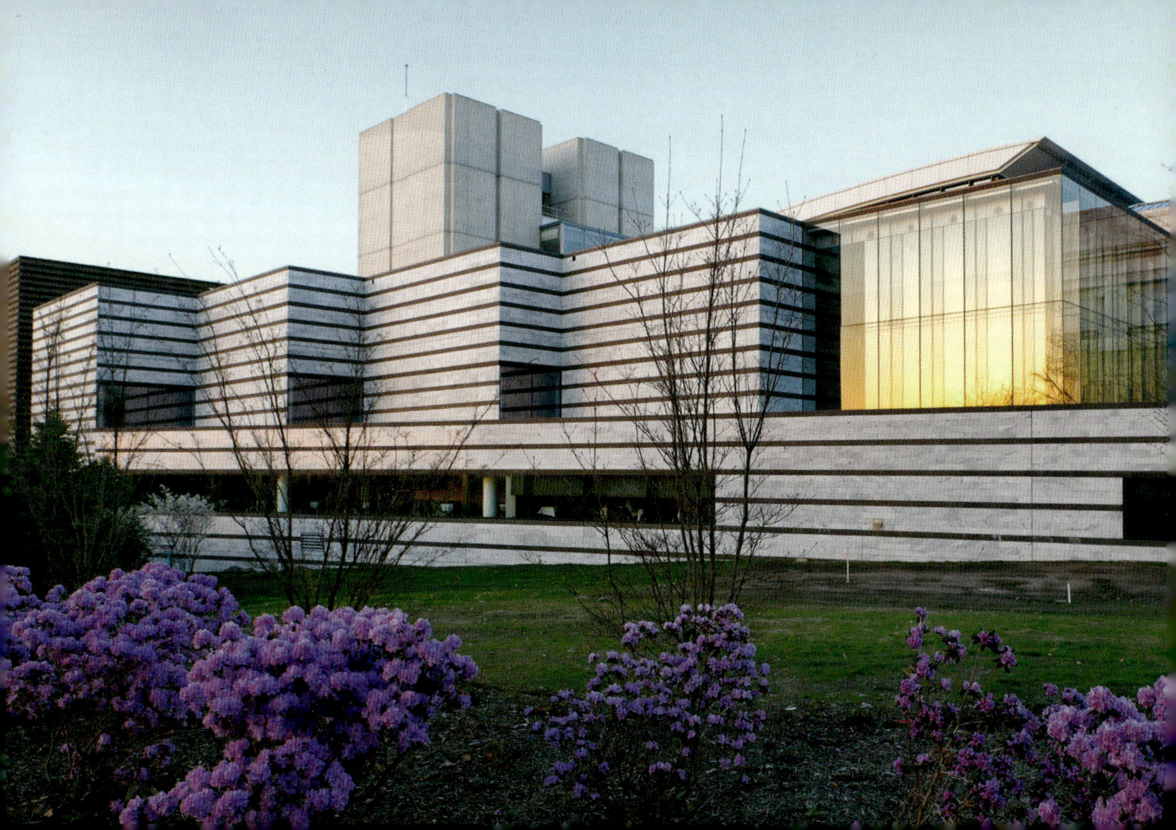

→ An ancient Costa Rican vessel in the Pre-Columbian galleries.

↓ Japanese art in the north galleries.

the form of two snakes and two birds. At the northern end of the Chinese area are paintings, decorative art, and ceramics.

The North Galleries

Moving from west to east in the north galleries, Chinese ceramics give way to Himalayan art. Korean art follows with objects including the eighth-century bronze *Stand-*

60 / THE CLEVELAND MUSEUM OF ART

Ingalls Library reading room. →

ing Buddha Amitabha and a Joseon period celadon storage jar. The art of Japan includes rotating installations of light-sensitive screens and scrolls, and Japanese sculpture highlights include the neolithic *Flame-Style Storage Vessel* and the thirteenth-century wooden *Portrait of the Zen Master Hotto Kokushi*. Two galleries of textiles mark the transition to the galleries of the art of the Americas. Mesoamerican art includes such works as the Maya ceramic *Vessel with Battle Scene* from Honduras and an Aztec *Figure of a Warrior* in solid gold. The final gallery features works from cultures centered in the ancient Andes, including the striking blue-and-yellow feathered panel featured in the recent exhibition *Wari: Lords of the Ancient Andes*.

The Next Century

The Cleveland Museum of Art is one of very few free museums that operate virtually without federal subsidy, and it is committed to remain available, free of charge, for present and future generations. Further, its historic approach of quality over quantity means that, unlike any

← Revelers crowd a family festival celebrating the opening of the atrium, 2012.

other collection of its caliber, the museum truly may be experienced in a single day (although, because admission is free, all visitors may come as often as they like). As the museum looks ahead to its next century, director David Franklin emphasizes that it is not his intention to increase the size of the museum. Instead, he charges curators with finding art so exceptional that something currently on view could move into storage. Such an approach has economic benefits as well as aesthetic ones. The commitment to caring for objects over the long term is the same no matter whether the works are good or great; because Cleveland already has a world-class collection, the focus should be on fewer objects but those of the highest quality. Thus the transformed museum's moderate physical scale is a virtue not only because it offers a manageable experience to visitors, but also because it allows the museum to operate more efficiently. These benefits—along with the surpassing beauty of its collection and the glorious architectural presentation—empower the museum in its mission to preserve and share with the public the greatest works of art for all posterity.

Visitors entering south doors at reopening → celebration for the 1916 building, 2008.

Text and images copyright © 2013 The Cleveland Museum of Art

This edition © 2013 Scala Arts Publishers, Inc.

First published in 2013 by
Scala Arts Publishers, Inc.
141 Wooster Street, Suite 4D
New York, NY 10012
www.scalapublishers.com

Scala Arts & Heritage Publishers Ltd.
21 Queen Anne's Gate
London SW1H 9BU
United Kingdom

Published in collaboration with
The Cleveland Museum of Art
11150 East Boulevard
Cleveland, OH 44106
www.ClevelandArt.org

Distributed outside the Cleveland Museum of Art in the book trade by Antique Collectors' Club
6 West 18th Street, Suite 4B
New York, NY 10011

ISBN: 978-1-85759-836-0
Library of Congress Control Number: 2013945436

All rights reserved. No part of the contents of this book may be reproduced, stored in a retrieval system, or transmitted in any form or by any means, electronic, mechanical, photocopying, recording, or otherwise, without the written permission of the Cleveland Museum of Art and Scala Arts Publishers, Inc.

Project management for Scala by Amy Pastan
Copy editor Ulrike Mills
Designed by Patricia Inglis

Front cover: The original 1916 building by Hubbell and Benes, and Rafael Viñoly's east wing addition seen from southeast.

Back cover: Sol LeWitt's *Wall Drawing 590a* seen from the north.

Every effort has been made to acknowledge copyright of images where applicable. Any errors of omission are unintentional and should be brought to the attention of the publishers.

Except where credited below, all photographs were produced by The Cleveland Museum of Art.

Illustration Credits

Cleveland Museum of Art photography: Howard T. Agriesti, David A. Brichford, and Gregory M. Donley.

Other illustration credits:

© Yvonne R. Anderson, courtesy the Cleveland Museum of Art: 17

The Cleveland Museum of Art Archives: 3–10

© Brad Feinknopf, courtesy Rafael Viñoly Architects: cover, 36–39, 40 (left), 45

© Focal Plane, courtesy the Cleveland Museum of Art: 25

© Jennie Jones Photography, courtesy the Cleveland Museum of Art: 20, 41 (bottom), back cover

© Stuart Pearl: 2, 59

© George Sexton Associates: 40 (right), 41 (top)

© Rafael Viñoly Architects: 13, 15, 16, 22–24